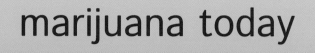

marijuana today

Marijuana in Society

marijuana today

The Benefits of Medical Marijuana:
from Cancer to PTSD

Growing Career Opportunities
in the Marijuana Industry

Marijuana: Facts, Figures, & Opinions

Marijuana in Society

Marijuana's Harmful Effects on Youth

marijuana today

Marijuana in Society

Julie Nelson

MASON CREST

Mason Crest
450 Parkway Drive, Suite D
Broomall, Pennsylvania 19008
(866) MCP-BOOK (toll-free)
www.masoncrest.com

First printing
9 8 7 6 5 4 3 2 1

ISBN (hardback) 978-1-4222-4105-9
ISBN (series) 978-1-4222-4103-5
ISBN (ebook) 978-1-4222-7693-8

Cataloging-in-Publication Data on file with the Library of Congress

NATIONAL
HIGHLIGHTS

Developed and Produced by National Highlights Inc.
Editor: Andrew Morkes
Proofreader: Mika Jin
Interior and cover design: Yolanda Van Cooten
Production: Michelle Luke

QR CODES AND LINKS TO THIRD-PARTY CONTENT

contents

KEY ICONS TO LOOK FOR:

Words to understand: These words with their easy-to-understand definitions will increase the reader's understanding of the text while building vocabulary skills.

Sidebars: This boxed material within the main text allows readers to build knowledge, gain insights, explore possibilities, and broaden their perspectives by weaving together additional information to provide realistic and holistic perspectives.

Educational Videos: Readers can view videos by scanning our QR codes, providing them with additional educational content to supplement the text. Examples include news coverage, moments in history, speeches, iconic sports moments and much more!

Text-dependent questions: These questions send the reader back to the text for more careful attention to the evidence presented there.

Research projects: Readers are pointed toward areas of further inquiry connected to each chapter. Suggestions are provided for projects that encourage deeper research and analysis.

Series glossary of key terms: This back-of-the-book glossary contains terminology used throughout this series. Words found here increase the reader's ability to read and comprehend higher-level books and articles in this field.

Introduction

Over the past twenty years, public views of marijuana have changed significantly in the United States, Canada, and other countries. What was once viewed as simply a recreational drug is now being considered a medical marvel by some scientists and members of the public. Research studies have shown that medical cannabis in various forms can be used to treat pain, nausea caused by cancer and other diseases, muscle spasms caused by multiple sclerosis, poor appetite and weight loss caused by chronic illness, seizure disorders, Crohn's disease, and other medical conditions. It is also being used to help fight post-traumatic stress disorder and the opioid abuse crisis. Despite the benefits of medical cannabis, there are continuing controversies over which illnesses and disorders can be treated with cannabis, and how real the effects reported in the news are. It's clear that more medical research must be conducted to fully understand the medical benefits of cannabis. Although this debate continues, many countries have approved its use. In the United States, twenty-nine states and the District of Columbia, Puerto Rico, and Guam now permit the use of medical cannabis. Other countries that have legalized medical cannabis in recent years include Canada, Mexico, Australia, Jamaica, Colombia, the Czech Republic, Spain, Portugal, Switzerland, Romania, Germany, India, Israel, Macedonia, South Africa, and Uruguay.

It is also clear that not everyone believes that cannabis should be legalized for recreational use. Many people still firmly believe that cannabis is a dangerous drug, and are opposed to recreational adult use. They cite an increase in traffic accidents in states that allow recreational cannabis use, the negative effects of cannabis on youth (although recreational users must be at least twenty-one), an increase in crime and threatening of moral values, and a rise in hospitalizations and marijuana-related poisonings. Despite the continuing controversy, eight states in the United States have legalized recreational cannabis for adult use: Alaska, California, Colorado, Maine,

Attitudes about the use of cannabis are changing around the world.

Vancouver, Canada, is referred to as the Amsterdam of North America. The Canadian government is currently in the process of legalizing cannabis for recreational use.

Massachusetts, Nevada, Oregon, and Washington. Recreational use of cannabis has been decriminalized in France, Denmark, Italy, Spain, United Kingdom, Czech Republic, Ireland, and Germany, although it is still technically illegal. The Netherlands has long allowed the use of medical cannabis (and has ignored recreational use), but recreational cannabis laws are becoming stricter in this European country.

Groundbreaking medical discoveries are only part of the new cannabis story, however; the revenue that medical and recreational cannabis businesses are generating across the board has become one of its most interesting aspects. Revenues in the U.S. legal cannabis market alone were $6.7 billion, as reported by the cannabis industry research firm Arcview Market Research. The U.S. cannabis industry employs 165,000 to 230,000 workers. It's estimated that the legal cannabis market will create more than a quarter of a million new jobs within three years. This is higher than the expected new jobs that will become available in manufacturing, utilities, or the government.

By the time you finish reading this book, you'll understand the important differences between tetrahydrocannabinol and cannabidiol, the different ways in which marijuana is now consumed, the benefits and drawbacks of cannabis use, and current developments in the medical and recreational legalization of cannabis in the United States and in countries around the world. We know so much more about marijuana today than we ever have before, and this book will help you to understand the science behind marijuana, public opinion and laws in the United States and in other countries, and how it has become a major business in the United States and around the world.

anesthetic: A drug that is used to prevent pain during surgery or other medical procedures.

deleterious: Something that is harmful.

opium: A highly addictive narcotic drug that is created by collecting and drying the milky juice that comes from the seed pods of the poppy plant.

prohibition: The action of forbidding something, especially by law.

propaganda: False information that is created to influence people.

psychoactive A drug that affects the mind.

chapter 1

Marijuana in the Past Century

Understanding Cannabis, Marijuana, and Hemp

Cannabis is the common name for *Cannabis sativa*, a green, leafy plant that is also known as *hemp*. Marijuana refers to the dried flowers, leaves, stems, and seeds of the cannabis plant. Cannabis is an annual herb with leafy, erect stems, elongated leaves in clusters of three to seven, and pistillate flowers that spike from its branches.

Hemp seed oil can be used to make non-toxic diesel fuel.

The term "cannabis" refers to both the marijuana plant and hemp, but the two plants are different. The flowers of the marijuana plant (which are also known as buds) contain a natural chemical compound called tetrahydrocannabinol (THC), which produces a feeling of euphoria and a **psychoactive** reaction (or "high") when eaten or smoked. Marijuana can also refer to other products of the psychoactive cannabis plant, including extracts, oils, and concentrates. (In this textbook, both plants are referred to as "cannabis," except where the terms "marijuana," "hemp," or "marijuana" are historically accurate or necessary.)

Hemp has been grown in what is now the United States since 1611, when European settlers arrived in the Jamestown settlement in the Colony of Virginia. These settlers were required by law to grow hemp, and penalized if they refused. Prior to the 1900s in the United States, hemp was made into textiles that were used for clothing, ship sails, and wagon coverings. It was a staple agricultural crop in the Americas prior to marijuana **prohibition** in the early 20th century. THC is present in only very small amounts in hemp, so consuming it will not produce a euphoric feeling. The growth of hemp is allowed on a state-by-state basis in the United States, and it is strictly regulated.

It is legal to grow industrial hemp in some countries such as China, France, Australia, and Canada, as well as in certain states in the United States. Industrial hemp produces as much fiber per acre as two to three acres of cotton and grows faster, according to HempBasics.com. Hemp is also stronger than cotton and lasts longer. Hemp fiber can be used to make paper, fiberboard, plastic substitutes, clothing and other textiles, and food and nutritional supplements. Hemp seed oil can be used to make non-toxic diesel fuel, paints and varnishes, inks, detergents, and lubricating oil.

View the 1936 trailer for the marijuana propaganda film Reefer Madness *to see how cannabis was depicted by the media and society in the 1930s.*

Cannabis Prior to 1937 in the United States

Cannabis was incorporated into medical practices and procedures in the 1800s (and used to treat inflammation, provide pain relief, and as an **anesthetic**), but a major

During World War II, American farmers were asked to grow hemp to aid in the war effort. Above, hemp rope was used during the manufacture of fighter jets.

shift began at the end of the 19th century. **Opium** addiction swept the world, and cannabis was targeted by the League of Nations as people began to question its use. In 1906, President Theodore Roosevelt signed the Pure Food and Drug Act. It required the labeling of all medicines including those containing marijuana. The act was designed to prevent the manufacture, sale, and transportation of "adulterated or misbranded or poisonous or **deleterious** foods, drugs, medicines, and liquors." Massachusetts regulated marijuana in 1911, followed quickly by Indiana, Maine, Wyoming, New York City, Utah, Vermont, Colorado, and Nevada. In 1914, President Woodrow Wilson signed the Harrison Narcotic Tax Act. When it went into effect in March 1915, the law limited the import and export of opium for medicinal purposes and imposed a tax on people who sold, distributed, or gave away opium or coca leaves.

A large number of Mexican immigrants coming into the United States during the Mexican Revolution (c. 1910–1920) fueled fear of Mexican culture and its marijuana use. In his book *Reefer Madness: Sex, Drugs, and Cheap Labor in the American Black Market*, Eric Schlosser noted that marijuana intoxication in Mexicans was frequently (and erroneously) associated with violent crime. Additionally, U.S. citizens began to negatively associate marijuana with West Indian immigrants, African-American jazz musicians, and criminal whites.

In 1930, Harry J. Anslinger, the commissioner of the Federal Bureau of Narcotics, and Henry J. Finger, a member of the California State Board of Pharmacy, agreed that the United States government should prohibit cannabis (Mexico had prohibited it a decade earlier). In 1936, the Federal Bureau of Narcotics officially recommended federal control of marijuana. Meanwhile, new pain medications such as aspirin and morphine were replacing marijuana. The Marihuana Tax Act, which was based on the Harrison Act, was passed in 1937. Cannabis farmers were required to register with the government and pay high taxes on their crops. The 1937 Marihuana Tax Act caused a decline in cannabis prescriptions in the U.S. and ultimately its prohibition Meanwhile, states continued to ban cannabis under the name of "marihuana."

This anti-drug film from the 1950s details the dangers of cannabis and heroin.

Cannabis Prohibition in the 20th Century

Following the implementation of the Marihuana Tax Act, cannabis use declined in the U.S., except during the "Hemp for Victory" campaign during World War II, when farmers were asked to grow hemp for the war effort. The Boggs Act (1952) and the

Narcotics Control Act (1956) established mandatory sentences for all drug-related offenders, including those who used marijuana. During the 1960s, cannabis was embraced by the youth counterculture, and it became more popular with the white upper middle class. In 1968, the Federal Bureau of Narcotics and the Bureau of Drug Abuse Control, an agency of the Food and Drug Administration, merged. In 1973, the U.S. Drug Enforcement Agency was formed, and, in 1986, President Ronald Reagan signed the Anti-Drug Abuse Act, which equated cannabis possession with heroin possession. Medical cannabis was legalized in California in 1996 to permit its use in the treatment of people with often terminal diseases such as cancer and AIDS.

The King of Cannabis Prohibition: Harry J. Anslinger

Harry J. Anslinger was the Commissioner of the Federal Bureau of Narcotics for thirty-two years. He strongly influenced the passage of the Marihuana Tax Act of 1937. Anslinger believed that young people were "slaves to this narcotic, continuing addiction until they deteriorate mentally, become insane, and turn to violent crime and murder." Anslinger was openly racist and opposed to marijuana. He linked black and Latino cultures with marijuana and claimed that cannabis use promoted interracial mixing and relationships, which he was against. Anslinger's opinions about cannabis soon became the beliefs of the majority of people in the United States.

The Legalization of Cannabis

Medical cannabis was legal in some countries such as the Netherlands prior to recent United States legalization, but California's bold move to allow gravely ill citizens to use cannabis set a precedent. As of 2017, twenty-nine states permitted the use of medical cannabis, and Guam, Puerto Rico, and the District of Columbia passed similar laws. Australia, Argentina, Chile, Israel, and more than twenty European countries have legalized medical cannabis as well.

Nearly thirty U.S. states and many countries have legalized the use of medical cannabis. Above, medical marijuana is displayed at a legal marijuana dispensary.

Famous Cannabis Advocates

Since medical cannabis was legalized in California in 1996, many celebrities have come forward to advocate for the legalization of cannabis, including musicians, actors, athletes, and other public figures. For example, musicians such as Willie Nelson and Snoop Dogg have produced their own cannabis and cannabis product lines. Celebrities such as Whoopi Goldberg, Bill Maher, and Lady Gaga also support cannabis legalization.

Recreational cannabis is somewhat less accepted across the world, but in the United States eight states have legalized it for adult consumption:

- Alaska
- California
- Colorado
- Maine
- Massachusetts
- Nevada
- Oregon
- Washington

The country musician Willie Nelson is a major supporter of cannabis legalization.

The new cannabis industry is often called the "green rush," echoing the U.S. gold rush in the mid-1800s. *Forbes* projects that the international market for non-psychoactive hemp oil (known as cannabidiol, or CBD) could grow by 700 percent by 2020. Cannabis sales in North America reached $6.7 billion in 2016, according to a report by Arcview Market Research. The use of CBD has reduced seizures in some patients with severe epilepsy as well as reduced the negative effects of other diseases and disorders. Advocates for further cannabis legalization cite a desire to use it to treat illnesses and disorders in a more natural, affordable, and healthy way. In the future, cannabis legalization may help prevent opioid addiction and other illnesses. In states that legalized medical marijuana, U.S. hospitals treated far fewer opioid users, according to a report in *Drug and Alcohol Dependence*. Hospitalization rates for opioid painkiller dependence and abuse declined 23 percent on average in states after marijuana was allowed for medicinal purposes. While many benefits have been associated with the use of cannabis, further study is required to determine the positive and negative effects of this drug.

The sale of legal cannabis at dispensaries such as the one pictured above has become big business in the United States and other countries.

1. How is marijuana different from hemp?
2. When was medical cannabis legalized in the United States?
3. What was Harry J. Anslinger's association with marijuana prohibition?

research project

Check out U.S. state medical marijuana laws at the National Conference of State Legislatures' website, http://www.ncsl.org/research/health/state-medical-marijua-na-laws.aspx. What are the medical marijuana laws in your state? What are the different limits of the laws? If you don't live in the United States, conduct research to determine what marijuana laws exist in your country.

The cannabis plant has more than seven hundred chemical compounds—some of which can be used for medical purposes.

words to understand

cannabinoid: Any of various chemical compounds (such as THC) from the cannabis or marijuana plant that produces a euphoric feeling, or "high."

delta-9-tetrahydrocannabinol (THC): A natural chemical compound found in the flowers of the marijuana plant. It produces a feeling of euphoria and a psychoactive reaction, or "high," when marijuana is eaten or smoked.

edible: A food made or infused (cooked or otherwise prepared) with cannabis extracts (portions of the plant, including seeds or flowers).

endocannabinoid system: A group of cannabinoid receptors found in the brain and central and peripheral nervous systems of mammals that help control appetite, pain, mood, and memory.

euphoria: A feeling of intense well-being and happiness.

tincture: A medicine made by dissolving a drug in alcohol, vinegar, or glycerites.

vaporizer: A device that is used to turn water or medicated liquid into a vapor for inhalation.

chapter 2

What Is Marijuana?

The Chemical Makeup of Marijuana

For years, marijuana has been the most commonly used illegal drug in the United States, according to the National Institute on Drug Abuse. But, now it is legal to use it for medical and recreational purposes in some U.S. states, as well as in some foreign countries. The cannabis plant—from which marijuana and hemp can be made depending on how the plant is bred—contains many different **cannabinoids**. Only a few have been synthesized (to make something chemically) in laboratories. Cannabinoids are chemical compounds that are present in the cannabis flower. When introduced to the body, they interact with areas of the brain and produce a euphoric feeling, or "high."

Smoking marijuana is one of the most common ways to consume the drug.

Among the cannabinoids created by the cannabis plant are **delta-9-tetrahydrocannabinol** (also known as THC); cannabidiol (CBD); cannabicyclol, cannabichromene, nabilone, tetrahydrocannabivarin, cannabigerol (CBG); tetrahydrocannabinolic acid; caryophyllene, 11-hydroxy-THC; and cannabidivarin. Of these, THC and CBD are currently of most interest to patients, scientists, and medical professionals.

THC is the cannabinoid that produces marijuana's psychoactive properties. CBD is the cannabinoid most valued for its medical benefits and pain relief properties. Cannabis affects the human body and mind by attaching, or binding, to the body's receptors (groups of specialized cells that can convert energy into electrical impulses), located in the **endocannabinoid system** (ECS). This system, which exists in human beings and in almost all animals, was discovered by Dr. Raphael Mechoulam, an Israeli organic chemist and professor of medicinal chemistry at Hebrew University of Jerusalem. Mechoulam completed a total synthesis of THC, CBD, CBG, and other cannabinoids beginning in 1964. His purpose in identifying and synthesizing the cannabinoids was to allow them to be used as medicines in the future. This has come to pass since Mechoulam's discoveries. The medicines Dronabinol, Marinol, and Nabilone are currently approved by the U.S. Food and Drug Administration (FDA) for treatment of patients with various illnesses, disorders, and health issues. Sativex, a cannabis-based spray created by GW Pharmaceuticals, is available in some European countries, but not currently in the United States.

Dr. Raphael Mechoulam, an Israeli scientist who discovered THC in cannabis and the endocannabinoid system, is pictured above (standing, second from left) at a gathering of the Israel Academy of Sciences and Humanities.

Common Side Effects of THC

Consuming marijuana, whether through inhaling or ingesting it, can cause the following common side effects in humans and in animals. These side effects are more noticeable in animals due to their often lower body weight.

- Increase in appetite
- Reduced motor control (coordination of the muscles and limbs)
- Increase or decrease in anxiety, fear, and emotion
- Increase in feelings of **euphoria** or relaxation
- Decrease in feeling pain
- Impaired thinking
- Shift in attentional focus
- Decrease in the ability to learn new tasks
- Decrease in the ability to regulate balance, posture, and coordination
- Decrease in reaction time

For these reasons, driving after using marijuana is never a good idea. More extreme side effects of consuming marijuana have been reported as well, although it's unclear if these side effects are a direct result of marijuana consumption or if people were affected by other circumstances.

What is THC?

The chemical structure of THC, the compound in marijuana that produces a euphoric feeling, or "high," is structurally similar to a chemical called anandamide that is naturally created by the human brain. Because THC is so similar to anandamide, the human body recognizes it as anandamide and produces identical effects when marijuana is ingested (to take food, drink, or another substance into the body).

Anandamide was also discovered by Raphael Mechoulam (in collaboration with William Devane). It is nicknamed the "bliss molecule." Anandamide is an endogenous (within the body) cannabinoid that acts like a neurotransmitter (a chemical that communicates information) in the brain, sending messages between neurons (nerve cells). THC produces its euphoric effects by binding to cannabinoid receptors in the endocannabinoid system of the body and brain. Endogenous cannabinoids affect pleasure, memory, movement, concentration, sensory perception, and time perception, thus producing the effects of the marijuana-induced "high." Consuming or inhaling marijuana produces side effects in the body, which may differ depending on the user. In general, THC causes neurons to release dopamine (a naturally occurring chemical in the human body). This increases pleasurable feelings in the mind and body.

What is CBD?

Cannabidiol, or CBD, is a chemical compound found in the cannabis plant. The main difference between THC and CBD is that CBD is non-psychoactive. This means that it does not create a "high" or feeling of euphoria in those who consume it. It is increasingly being used to help relieve pain, inflammation, and nausea, as well as reduce anxiety, although scientists continue to study the potentially positive and negative

Charlotte Figi, The Stanley Brothers, and Charlotte's Web

The story of Charlotte Figi is an excellent example of the seizure-reducing effects of CBD oil (an oil extracted from the hemp plant). She is a girl from Colorado who suffers from Dravet syndrome, a severe form of pediatric epilepsy that often causes prolonged and frequent seizures accompanied by issues with sensory integration, growth and nutrition, movement and balance, and behavior and development. In 2013, a family of cannabis growers and breeders known as the Stanley Brothers answered Charlotte's mother's request to help create a medicine for Charlotte, whose seizures were so severe she was often near death. Traditional medicines did not work for Charlotte, who was having upwards of four hundred seizures per week. Her mother had to perform CPR twice on her to save her life. The Stanley Brothers created what became known as Charlotte's Web, a strain of cannabis just for Charlotte, extracting the CBD and creating an oil with no euphoric effects. The change in Charlotte was dramatic. After daily treatment with CBD extract, her seizures all but disappeared, greatly improving her quality of life. While the results of CBD therapy for those suffering from epileptic disorders are not always as effective as Charlotte's treatment (and some-times may be more effective), the degree of seizure reduction is often so dramatic that families travel hundreds of miles just to try CBD oil for their children. Charlotte's Web is most commonly used today to prevent pediatric epilepsy. Since this discovery, CBD has been proven through preclinical trials to be an anti-inflam-matory, a neuroprotectant (a substance that repairs and protects the nervous system, its cells, structure, and function), and a pain reliever (or analgesic). The CBD extract market is now booming in the United States, Canada, and other countries, as further effects of CBD continue to be studied in medical trials.

effects of the compound. CBD is also being used to help treat seizures and other neurological disorders. For example, a Colorado-based family known as the Stanley Brothers pioneered a non-psychotropic cannabis variety, or strain, of cannabis in 2012 that has been extremely successful in reducing seizures for children suffering from various types of severe pediatric epilepsy, such as Dravet syndrome and Lennox-Gastaut syndrome. Epilepsy is a disorder of the brain that causes seizures, a sudden surge of electrical activity in the brain that affects how a person behaves or feels for a short time. Some seizures occur frequently and some hardly at all. They affect people differently and are not well controlled by traditional medications in many cases (this is called treatment-resistant epilepsy). For treatment-resistant epilepsy, the alternatives may be invasive surgery (in which a cut, or incision, is made in the body and instruments or other medical devices are inserted to perform a procedure) or even having the patient participate in clinical trials (experiments with unproven medications that may or may not help a patient get better) aimed at using new medicines to reduce seizures.

ONLY ON 7NEWS
PRODUCTION EXPANDED FOR CHARLOTTE'S WEB
MEDICAL CANNABIS WILL SOON BE MORE WIDELY AVAILABLE

Learn more about Charlotte Figi and Charlotte's Web.

Methods of Marijuana Consumption

Marijuana consumption is most often achieved by smoking or vaporizing the plant material itself, or an extract of the plant material. However, eating or drinking marijuana may cause more noticeable and longer-lasting effects. It's important to

The Cannabis-Infused Marketplace

Cannabis-infused products have become very popular among cannabis users because they are discreet, or not as obvious to others as smoking a marijuana cigarette. Additionally, users believe that they greatly improve the experience of eating, drinking, and being social. Due to the sensory effects (vision, hearing, smell, etc.) of cannabis, growth in the marijuana edibles and beverages sector is strong. Options for cannabis-infused products range from brownies and cookies to chocolate-covered coffee beans, wines, and beers. These products often cost more than traditional plant-material cannabis does. The Arcview Group, a cannabis business research firm, noted that "concentrates and edibles are becoming customer favorites versus traditional smoking," and California reported $180 million in cannabis-infused edibles sales in 2016. In Washington, cannabis-infused products sales increased 121 percent in 2016. Cannabis edibles can, however, produce very strong effects, and have been linked to increased feelings of depression in some users. The Mayo Clinic reports that cannabis use can trigger detachment from reality, also known as psychosis, in those who have been diagnosed with mental illness. Cannabis edible distributors in Colorado are now required to place warnings on packaging, indicating the time they may need to take effect, and proper dosage. While the link between mental illness and cannabis use has not been proven scientifically due to limits on cannabis use in medical trials in the United States, cannabis consumers with a history of mental illness, as well as those using cannabis for the first time, should be very cautious.

remember that recreational cannabis should only be used by adults as appropriate under the laws of their city, state, province, or country, and medical cannabis should only be given to children after consultation between their parents and medical professionals.

Inhaling Marijuana

Medical studies have determined that inhaling marijuana smoke is harmful to the lungs just as inhaling tobacco smoke is. That is, it causes "visible and microscopic injury to the large airways," according to a 2013 study published in the *Annals of the American Thoracic Society*. But there is no indication that this damage is permanent. In fact, in the same study, researchers found that there was "no clear link" to lung diseases such as chronic obstructive pulmonary disease, and there was a possible increase in lung function for marijuana smokers who do not smoke cigarettes. Thus, although marijuana smoking can damage parts of the lungs (the bronchial epithelial ciliary and the alveolar macrophages), the researchers in this study could not find a clear link between lower respiratory tract infection and marijuana use. The study concluded that tobacco smoke is far worse for the lungs than marijuana smoke. Still, inhaling burning hot marijuana smoke temporarily damages the lungs, makes people cough, and can be painful. And long-term, heavy intake of marijuana smoke is certainly not good for the lungs. The association between smoking marijuana and lung cancer remains unclear, according to the Alcohol & Drug Abuse Institute at the University of Washington. Some well-designed and large-scale studies have failed to identify any increased risk of lung cancer in people who have smoked marijuana. But the institute reports that "no study has definitively ruled out the possibility that some individuals, especially heavier marijuana users, may incur an elevated risk of cancer. This risk appears to be smaller than for tobacco, yet is important to consider when weighing the benefits and risks of smoking marijuana." It's clear that more research on the effects of marijuana smoking on the respiratory system is needed.

Vaporizing Marijuana

Cooling marijuana smoke with water is a popular way to reduce coughing for regular users. The most popular method today of consuming cooled marijuana smoke is called vaporizing. **Vaporizers** are devices that vaporize cannabis at a temperature in the range of 356 to 392 degrees Fahrenheit (180 to 200°C)—much lower than the temperature of fire that combusts (to be consumed by fire) marijuana plant material when it is smoked. The lower temperature releases the cannabinoids of cannabis material or cannabis-derived oil from the plant without creating ash and tar (a toxic byproduct of cigarette or marijuana smoking). Due to the lower temperature of vapor produced by these devices, the burning sensation of smoking cannabis or tobacco is eliminated and the lungs are less damaged than they might be if the marijuana were burned.

Vaporizers range in size from large, tabletop devices to discreet, hand-held devices about the size and shape of an expensive pen. Vaporizer pens, or portable vaporizers, are generally rechargeable and use a high-frequency ultrasonic vibration to turn cannabis into vapor. The heater used is called an atomizer, and it runs on batteries. Vaporizers can be used with marijuana plant material, such as the cola (or flower) and leaf, as well as oils. The marijuana vaporizer market is a fast-growing industry that generates a lot of money for vaporizer manufacturers and sellers.

The most popular method today of consuming cooled marijuana smoke is called vaporizing. A water pipe (pictured above) is used in this process.

Cannabis edibles—such as this chocolate marijuana cake with marijuana green butter—are popular because they allow users to avoid the inhalation risks of smoking or vaping.

Dabbing

Dabbing is a somewhat controversial method of cannabis flash-vaporization. It has very strong effects on the user. For dabbing, cannabis concentrates such as shatter (cannabis concentrate that looks like colored glass), wax, and CBD oil are placed onto a glass or metal "nail" that is heated up with fire and then inhaled. This method of cannabis consumption allows users to avoid experiencing the intense burning sensation of smoking. The intensity of the psychoactive effects from dabbing marijuana concentrates can be too strong for many people. They may produce a higher tolerance for marijuana and greater withdrawal side effects in users.

Edibles

Cannabis-infused foods and drinks are also very popular because they allow users to avoid the inhalation risks of smoking or "vaping." With some plant material or oil, many different foods and beverages can be infused with the effects of THC or CBD, causing the same euphoric or symptom-reducing effects of the smoked plant. Creating a THC-infused or CBD-infused recipe is simple if access to the ingredients is legal. However, the process of cooking with marijuana can increase its psychoactivity and affect users very differently. Additionally, feelings of euphoria usually last much longer than what occurs when inhaling through a vaping or smoking process. When consuming **edibles**, the euphoric effects are often stronger, and may take longer to become apparent. This has led to inexperienced or new marijuana edibles users eating too much of an edible. Doing so can lead to intense psychoactive effects that may frighten people or change their behavior dramatically. Today, all legally sold cannabis-infused products must be labelled with dosages (the correct amount to take) and THC concentrations.

Tinctures & Oils

A **tincture** is a type of medicine that is made by dissolving a drug in alcohol—although vinegar or glycerites are sometimes used. (Glycerites are the fluid extract of an herb or other medicinal substance that is made using glycerin.) Herbal tinctures have been used for thousands of years, and are used to extract and distill helpful plant materials by soaking the plant material in liquids. Alcohol tinctures take time to prepare, generally at least two weeks, and often use strong grain alcohol.

Cannabis oil can be consumed in food, directly placed in a capsule or under the tongue, or simply dropped into the mouth.

The simplest way to make a tincture is to soak plant material in a strong alcohol such as vodka. Tinctures are very popular in the medicinal cannabis industry. Water-based tinctures are not as effective at pulling cannabis oils into liquid as alcohol because water and oil do not mix. Creating an alcohol-based tincture from the cannabis plant results in a liquid that mixes well with water, however, which is why many tinctures are used in cooking or teas by cannabis users.

CBD, or cannabidiol, is most commonly consumed as an oil. It is extracted from the hemp plant and placed in either capsule form or combined with foods or drinks. This method of ingesting cannabinoids does not damage the lungs or any other part of the body. Tinctures enter the bloodstream much faster than oils and are usually placed under the tongue. They can be extremely bitter, so placing them under the tongue allows for easier consumption. Tinctures' effects are much faster than those of oils, and this allows better dosage control.

Cannabis oil extraction is now a scientific process that allows faster, more efficient production of large amounts of cannabis oil from large amounts of plant material. CBD oil is the medicine that children suffering from severe epilepsy diseases and

Cannabis ointments can be used to relieve pain and inflammation.

disorders often use to combat life-threatening seizures, as in the case of Charlotte Figi, mentioned earlier in the chapter. CBD oil can be consumed in food, directly placed in a capsule or under the tongue, or simply dropped directly into the mouth to reduce seizures and other symptoms associated with Dravet syndrome and other medical conditions.

Topicals

Topicals are cannabis-infused lotions, balms, and salves that relieve pain and aches at the application site on the body. They are made to reduce inflammation in a specific area, and are free of psychoactive effects, as well. Cannabis topicals are a way to take advantage of cannabis's pain-relieving properties without having to ingest the cannabis. Topicals allow some cannabinoids to enter the skin (known as the epidermis). However, they are not psychoactive and at most may lead to a feeling of relaxation, and relief from muscle cramping, headaches, and insomnia. Cannabis topicals often include other pain-relieving aromatic herbs such as eucalyptus or ginseng, and provide local relief of pain wherever they are placed on the body. Topicals work by absorbing into the skin, eventually penetrating the nerves that signal pain to the brain.

text-dependent questions

1. What are two cannabinoids present in cannabis?
2. How does THC affect the human body and mind?
3. How does a vaporizer work?

research project

Search the internet for scientific information about cannabidiol, and find three medical studies from scholarly journals. What did you learn after reading the studies?

words to understand

adult-use cannabis: The recreational use of cannabis by those over the age of twenty-one.

decriminalization: The legal term for getting rid of or reducing criminal charges for having or using cannabis.

lethargy: Lack of enthusiasm and energy; a common side effect of cannabis use.

medical cannabis identification card: A document issued by a state where it is legal to use medical cannabis; the card indicates that a patient may use, buy, or have medical cannabis at home, on his or her person, or both.

recreational cannabis use: The use of cannabis in social settings, whether in public or private.

chapter 3

Medical and Recreational Marijuana

Medical Marijuana Use

Marijuana has been used for medicinal purposes for thousands of years. After years of being outlawed in most countries, governments are recognizing the medical research that shows the value of medical marijuana in treating pain, nausea, muscle spasms, tremors, weight loss, poor appetite, and other symptoms of diseases and conditions such as cancer, multiple sclerosis, acquired immune deficiency syndrome, severe seizure disorders, Parkinson's disease, nerve pain and disorders, and Crohn's disease. Scientists are also studying the use of cannabis to treat post-traumatic stress disorder and opioid abuse (the misuse of prescription opioids and the use of heroin, an illegal drug). Early studies have shown that medical marijuana legalization may be associated with decreased prescription opioid abuse and overdose deaths.

In France, the use of medical cannabis derivatives is legal for patients with a prescription from a licensed doctor.

These medical benefits, growing interest in the use of herbal remedies and healthier diets and lifestyles to improve health and fight disease, and changes in the perception of cannabis by many people are fueling interest in medical marijuana.

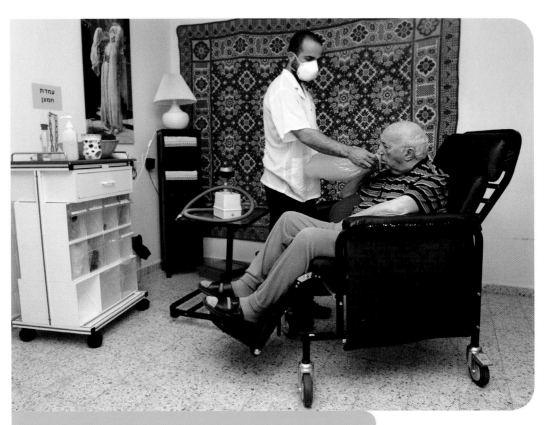

A man smokes medical marijuana in a special clinic in Israel.

While many effects of medical cannabis have yet to be medically and scientifically proven, trials and studies are ongoing in the areas of post-traumatic stress disorder, epilepsy, and other medical conditions. In the meantime, the use of medical cannabis is now legal in twenty-nine states and the District of Columbia, Guam, and Puerto Rico. It is also legal in Canada, Australia, The Netherlands, France, Israel, and other countries.

Benefits

In 2015, the World Health Organization (WHO) updated its Expert Committee on Drug Dependence definition of cannabis and medical uses, finding that the cannabis plant contains at least 750 chemicals, including 104 different cannabinoids.

Some of these chemical and cannabinoids provide medical benefits. The medical uses of cannabis are detailed in the update, including use of cannabinoid therapeutic applications such as in the medications Dronabinol, Marinol, and Nabilone, which are currently approved by the U.S. Food and Drug Administration (FDA) for treatment of patients with various illnesses, disorders, and health issues.

The Opioid Epidemic

Opioid abuse has become a major issue in the United States and around the world. Opioid abuse claims ninety-one American lives per day, according to the Centers for Disease Control and Prevention. This includes overdoses from prescription opioids and heroin. It also reports that over the past eighteen years, opioid prescription overdoses have quadrupled. More than six out of ten drug overdoses in the U.S. are opioid-related.

The medical effects of cannabis are the result of the cannabinoid bond with CB1 and CB2 receptors (groups of specialized cells that can convert energy into electrical impulses), in the human body in the endocannabinoid system. WHO found that these receptors are particularly concentrated in certain areas of the brain and body. For instance, the areas of the brain most affected by cannabis use include those that control cognition (gathering and understanding information), coordination, learning and memory, emotion, reward, appetite and sexual behavior, and nausea or pain.

WHO has recognized the need to re-examine the role of cannabis in human health in the wake of positive news regarding cannabis clinical trials and treatments. WHO also addresses the possible applications for CBD, and non-psychoactive phytocannabinoids like it, including treatment for psychosis, affective disorders, seizure disorders, inflammation, and neurodegenerative diseases. WHO observed that cannabis might be used to treat drug- and therapy-resistant diseases and disorders, such as Crohn's disease, chronic pain, cancer, or Alzheimer's disease.

Check out an interview with a medical cannabis farmer.

There are still more studies and work to be done before the U.S. medical community is comfortable recommending marijuana for patients. Federal laws in the United States often make in-depth cannabis research difficult for researchers because they conflict with state laws. Many cannabis organizations in the United States are trying to fully legalize cannabis at the federal level, and with the financial backing of many in the booming cannabis industry, they should be gaining more and more ground. Overall, there is a significant trend toward the acceptance of medical marijuana worldwide. However, the acceptance and promotion of medical cannabis depends on the views of the political party that is in power and the amount of government funding that is provided for research.

Drawbacks

Marijuana can and does have side effects, and often those side effects depend on the person consuming the plant, whether in marijuana form or in an infused bakery item. There is often no predicting how marijuana or a marijuana-derived product such as an edible might affect an individual. People also have varying reactions to over-the-counter drugs and prescriptions, as well. Although a current, FDA-approved medical trial is studying marijuana's ability to reduce symptoms of post-traumatic stress disorder such as anxiety, not everyone experiences a reduction in anxiety with marijuana use. Studies have found that while low doses of tetrahydrocannabinol (THC, a natural chemical compound found in the flowers of the marijuana plant) can reduce stress and anxiety, there is a threshold—meaning that a higher dose may cause more anxiety in the user.

While there have been no reported fatal overdoses from cannabis alone, in combination with other substances such as cocaine, alcohol, or heroin, death can occur. It's important to keep in mind that even prescription drugs have risks and can cause deaths. In the United States, for example, the American Association of Poison Control Centers estimates that about 113 people die each year as a result of overdosing on medicines that contain acetaminophen (a common pain reliever and fever reducer).

The Entourage Effect

Some medical cannabis users would prefer to experience fewer psychoactive effects when taking cannabis-based medicines. This is why CBD extraction is such a popular discovery in the realm of medical cannabis. However, there is a scientific theory called the entourage effect that argues that THC and non-psychoactive cannabinoids such as CBD work together to provide specific effects when combined in certain amounts. In other words, use of the whole plant together, instead of extracting certain cannabinoids like CBD, results in more efficient health effects that can be directed toward providing a specific experience or health benefit through chemistry. Scientists are not sure that the entourage effect is real, however. CBD is known to block the effects of THC, so in theory, when both are combined at a certain concentration, the user will not feel the effects of the THC even if it is there. Sativex, a cannabis-based medicine that is approved in more than twenty-five countries (but not the United States), contains the same amounts of THC and CBD. On the other hand, Marinol and Syndros, two cannabinoid therapeutic applications that are approved by the Food and Drug Administration, contain only THC dissolved in sesame seed oil and alcohol.

Studies have found that low doses of THC, a natural chemical compound found in the flowers of the marijuana plant, can reduce stress and anxiety. But using too much cannabis can cause more anxiety.

The side effects from heavy use of cannabis have been studied in more detail since these types of studies reinforced cannabis's illegality throughout the twentieth century. Research indicates that the negative side effects experienced from cannabis use are caused by THC, the compound in marijuana that produces a euphoric feeling or "high." Negative side effects that may occur after using cannabis include:

- **Lethargy**
- Impaired thinking
- Shift in attentional focus
- Decrease in the ability to learn new tasks
- Decrease in the ability to regulate balance, posture, and coordination
- Decrease in reaction time
- Increase in anxiety, fear, and emotion
- Possible psychotic episodes in people already diagnosed with mental illnesses

When it's used on a regular basis, cannabis users can experience withdrawal symptoms after stopping, including irritability, anxiety, restlessness, aggression, and sleep difficulties, according to a 2011 medical study on the negative, or adverse, effects of cannabis. The same study, however, points out that the "long-term effects of cannabis are difficult to evaluate," since it is often used in combination with other substances such as tobacco, alcohol, and illegal drugs.

Measuring Marijuana Intoxication

Driving while intoxicated with cannabis is a serious problem because marijuana use slows human reaction time, making split-second decisions more difficult. The police want to deter people from driving under the influence of cannabis, but a way to measure intoxication has not existed until recently. Urine and hair tests can detect cannabis use over a period of days or weeks, but they cannot be used to determine cannabis intoxication during a roadside test. Companies are working to create such a device. For example, Hound Labs in the United States and Cannabix Technologies in Canada have developed small handheld breathalyzer devices. These are similar to the alcohol impairment measurement devices currently used by police to measure alcohol intoxication in drivers. In the near future, police and other law enforcement agencies and substance abuse programs may use these devices to measure a person's THC-intoxication and determine whether it played a role in causing an auto accident or death.

Recreational Marijuana Use

Marijuana was used recreationally for many years in the United States before individual states started banning it in the early 1900s. Since marijuana has become legal for medical or recreational use in some U.S. states and other countries, many people have become more open about their cannabis use. In states where cannabis is recreationally legal, people may eat edibles and go to public places or be seen using cannabis in a vaporizer or joint form in public. All states where **recreational cannabis** is legal still have laws prohibiting public use, but in states such as Colorado, it is too difficult to tell whether cannabis or tobacco is being used in these situations. Law enforcement officers often look the other way at public events because other types of crime are more pressing or dangerous to the public.

Consuming cannabis can cause impaired thinking and a decrease in reaction time. For that reason, people should never drive a vehicle after using cannabis.

Recreational cannabis users are those who consume cannabis only for the THC high, the experience, or as part of a recreational activity—like having a drink with coworkers at a bar. Recreational cannabis use is considered non-medical, and is opposed by anti-cannabis groups and governments that do not support cannabis legalization. Recreational use includes all methods of cannabis ingestion, and refers to any non-medical use of the plant, its material, or extracts. Recreational cannabis use is generally centered around high-THC strains, social consumption of cannabis, and, unfortunately, driving while under the influence of cannabis, because marijuana use slows human reaction time, making split-second decisions more difficult.

Recreational cannabis use is legal in eight states: Colorado, Washington, Oregon, Alaska, California, Massachusetts, Maine, and Nevada, as well as in Washington, D.C. Colorado and Washington are often considered models for recreational cannabis use because they were the first states to legalize adult use in 2012. Alaska and Oregon soon followed in 2014, and California, Nevada, Maine, and Massachusetts legalized the use of recreational cannabis in 2016.

The recreational use of cannabis has been decriminalized in France, Denmark, Italy, Spain, United Kingdom, Czech Republic, Ireland, and Germany, although it is still technically illegal. The Canadian government is currently in the process of legalizing cannabis for recreational purposes. Medical use is already legal there. In Latin America, Uruguay has legalized medical and recreational cannabis.

Benefits

Beyond the enjoyment and health benefits it brings those over the age of twenty-one, **adult-use cannabis** legalization has provided a much-needed economic boom to Colorado, Nevada, Massachusetts, and other states, as well as other countries. People wishing to work in the legal cannabis industries in these states, or self-medicate with cannabis, are moving to legal adult-use states in record numbers. Much of the political platform of cannabis legalization was based on the promise of high tax revenues from cannabis and cannabis products. These revenues are then used to pay for educational needs; the repair or construction of roads, bridges, and other infrastructure; information campaigns on safe cannabis use; and programs that help people to stop abusing drugs.

The economic benefits of legalized cannabis are clear. For example, Colorado's cannabis revenue (including medical and adult-use cannabis) was over $1 billion two months before the end of 2016. The Colorado Department of Revenue reports that there are more than 470 medical and recreational cannabis dispensaries in Colorado, not including cultivation facilities that supply medical-grade and recreational cannabis to dispensaries; product manufacturers who create cannabis edibles, topicals, and tinctures; and testing facilities and labs. Transportation and security businesses are also thriving in legal medical and recreational states. Cannabis users in all legal adult-use states may consume in the privacy of their homes and on their own property, as long as they are not bothering their neighbors. In Colorado, cannabis private events are also legal, at which cannabis can be used openly prior to, during, or following an event. In recreationally legal states, a consumer must be twenty-one or older to purchase cannabis, and it is illegal to give or sell cannabis to minors. In many states, consumers may also grow a limited number of personal use cannabis plants, or cannabis for medical use for another patient. These growers may or may not require a license, depending on the number of plants being cultivated. Public use of cannabis is illegal in publicly-accessible areas such as schools, amusement parks, sporting venues, music venues, parks, playgrounds, and restaurants and bars (including patios).

The use of medical cannabis is legal in twenty-nine U.S. states. Cannabis is sold by medical marijuana dispensaries.

Drawbacks

Despite the popularity of legalized recreational cannabis, some people do not enjoy using cannabis, do not want their families affected by its use, and do not want to be around it. In general, cannabis use in legalized recreational states is much the same as alcohol use. It may happen in public places, and the frequency of use is high enough that in legal states, a person may witness cannabis use in public places despite the laws.

Driving while intoxicated by marijuana (as well as by alcohol and illegal and prescription drugs) continues to be a significant problem. Studies show that traffic accidents have increased in states or other areas that permit the recreational use of cannabis. In Colorado, for example, marijuana-related traffic deaths increased by 154 percent from 2006 to 2014, according to a report from the Rocky Mountain High Intensity Drug Trafficking Area, but it is difficult to know whether marijuana use caused the accidents, or whether the accidents happened for other reasons. A Highway Loss Data Institute report found that Colorado, Oregon, and Washington had a 3 percent increase in vehicle crashes, with individual crash reports in each state up a few percentage points. In Colorado, collision claims since marijuana legalization are up 16 percent. Police officers currently have no way to effectively measure cannabis impairment in drivers except a breathalyzer that was recently rolled out in Los Angeles.

Marijuana Use in the United States

More adults in the United States are using marijuana for medical and recreational purposes because it has become legal—especially for medical uses—in many states. In fact, nearly two hundred million Americans live in states where the use of cannabis is legal in some way, according to The Pew Charitable Trusts. It's hard to provide reliable usage statistics because the number of cannabis users prior to legalization was largely unknown because it was illegal, and because many current cannabis users may not report their use because of fear of losing their jobs or other forms of retribution, concerns about privacy, or fear of judgement by their peers.

How Many Americans Use Cannabis?

A 2017 poll by Yahoo News and Marist Poll found that 52 percent of U.S. adults had used cannabis in some shape or form, and, of those, 44 percent still used cannabis. Of those who have tried marijuana in the United States, 65 percent were parents, 30 percent were parents with children under the age of eighteen, and 63 percent used marijuana regularly. Another poll, this time by Gallup, found that 45 percent of Americans have tried marijuana, and 12 percent currently use it. This means that one in eight people currently use marijuana, and the poll also found that younger, lower-income men are the most likely to use cannabis. These are the highest numbers of reported marijuana use since 1969.

How Many Americans Use Medical Cannabis?

Since medical cannabis and recreational cannabis are currently legal in eight states, it is difficult within those states to separate medical use from recreational use. Many people self-medicate (treat themselves without getting advice from a doctor) with cannabis and are not required to buy medical cannabis. The *San Diego Union-Tribune* reports that 85,370 medical cannabis cards were issued to California residents from 2004 to 2016, but the National Organization for the Reform of Marijuana Laws states that 750,000 to 1.1 million people in California are medical marijuana patients in the state who may or may not have received their **medical cannabis identification cards.** The Marijuana Policy Project estimates that more than 2.3 million people in the United States are medical cannabis patients in legal medical cannabis states.

Global Marijuana Use

The World Health Organization (WHO) reports that cannabis is "by far the most widely cultivated, trafficked, and abused illicit drug." Half of all drug seizures across the planet are of cannabis, and nearly every country in the world has cannabis trafficking. WHO estimates that 147 million people, or 2.5 percent of the world population, consume cannabis annually. That is more than cocaine (.2 percent) and opiates (.2 percent) combined. Incidents of cannabis abuse have risen since the 1960s in developed countries such as Australia, Canada, France, Germany, and the United States. It has become "more closely linked to youth culture" as well.

In 2017, Israel **decriminalized** the use of cannabis for recreational purposes. It was also among the first countries in the world to legalize medical marijuana. Justice Minister Ayelet Shaked stated that "it is wrong to judge cannabis users per criminal law…the State of Israel cannot turn a blind eye in light of changes worldwide regarding cannabis consumption and effect." Other countries that have decriminalized cannabis to some degree or legalized it include:

- The Netherlands
- Mexico
- Czech Republic
- Costa Rica
- Portugal

- Colombia
- Ecuador
- Peru
- Spain
- Uruguay

Decriminalization does not mean that recreational cannabis is completely legal. Public use or possession of cannabis is allowed in certain amounts determined by each country, but strict criminal laws are no longer enforced in these countries. A small fine may be imposed for the first cannabis possession or use offense, followed by larger fines and possible prison time if cannabis is found or used repeatedly in public by the same offender. Overall, cannabis use has become much more acceptable in North America, Latin America, Mexico, Canada, Western Europe, and other countries and regions over the past twenty years. This trend is expected to continue during the next decade.

It is against the law to use cannabis in Indonesia. Above, police hold a press conference to show a large amount of cannabis that was taken away from drug dealers.

text-dependent questions

1. Approximately how many people across the planet use cannabis regularly?
2. What are some of the negative side effects of using cannabis?
3. Which U.S. states allow legal recreational cannabis use?

research project

Talk to your parents about cannabis use. Do they approve of it? In which situations? Has your parents' viewpoint on cannabis changed since its use has become legal in some U.S. states and in other countries?

Recreational use of cannabis has been permitted in The Netherlan[d] since the 1970s. Above, cannabis infused candy and cookies are offered for sale in a coffee shop i[n] Amsterdam.

words to understand

cannabis clubs: Marijuana growing and consumption cooperatives (a group that is owned and run by its members) that exist in countries such as Uruguay and Spain to provide cannabis users with marijuana products and a place to use those products.

decriminalization: Reducing or getting rid of punishments for the possession and use of small amounts of cannabis.

drug trafficking: A global illegal trade involving the growth, manufacture, distribution, and sale of substances, such as cannabis, that are subject to drug prohibition laws.

neurodegenerative diseases: An umbrella term for conditions that primarily affect the brain neurons (nerve cells); they are incurable and make people weak and infirm.

War on Drugs: An anti-drug campaign started in the United States in 1971 by then-president Richard Nixon. Its goal was to fight drug abuse and shipments of illegal drugs to the U.S. from Latin America, Mexico, and other places.

chapter 4

Marijuana Around the World

Global Marijuana

The legalization of cannabis by some U.S. states is big news these days, but cannabis has been legal or **decriminalized** in some countries for decades. For example, the recreational use of cannabis has been decriminalized in France, Denmark, Italy, Spain, United Kingdom, Czech Republic, Ireland, and Germany, although it is still technically illegal. The Netherlands has long allowed the use of medical cannabis (and has ignored recreational usage). The use of cannabis is illegal in China, but it has a large legal hemp industry. Israel has allowed and funded medical marijuana research for years, and decriminalized the use of small amounts of cannabis in 2017. Uruguay has legalized medical and recreational cannabis, and Mexico and some countries in

In the United States, recreational use of cannabis increased during the 1960s as liberal viewpoints became more popular. San Francisco (especially the neighborhood around the cross streets of Haight and Ashbury) became a popular destination for cannabis users.

The Cannabis Black Market

Despite legalization, the cannabis black market still exists, even in the United States where many people now have access to medical or recreational marijuana. **Drug trafficking** still occurs on a large scale across the world, although recent legalization measures and efforts have increasingly affected the Mexican drug cartels, which are responsible for a large amount of violence. In states where marijuana is still illegal, legal marijuana is purchased from other states and brought back to sell on the black market. Marijuana legalization proponents believe that one way to help eliminate the black market for cannabis is to legalize it at the federal level. Senator Cory Booker of New Jersey has introduced legislation to do exactly that. Supporters of this proposed law believe that legalizing cannabis at the federal level will allow the marijuana market to be fully controlled (or regulated), allowing for better quality, more reasonable pricing, and more supply for consumer demand.

Latin America are beginning to support legalization. Understanding cannabis laws in different countries, as well as their residents' views about cannabis, can lead to a greater understanding of cannabis, its place in different cultures, and the future of legalized medical and recreational cannabis.

The Netherlands

Prior to the current U.S. legalization trend, Amsterdam, the capital of the Netherlands, was one of the most popular places for cannabis consumers to go to publicly use marijuana. Beginning in 1976, law enforcement officials began to allow cannabis use, essentially decriminalizing up to five grams (0.17637 ounces) of personal use cannabis. In Amsterdam, this openness toward cannabis use—which was called *gedoogbeleid*—led to the opening of more than three hundred "coffee shops" in Amsterdam, where visitors or citizens could smoke marijuana without being arrested. Seven hundred more such shops operated in other parts of the Netherlands, according to *Newsweek*. In the past, Amsterdam was considered one of the most tolerant cities for marijuana consumption, and use of other drugs was often ignored, as well. But, today, Amsterdam has begun to change its policies after decades of "looking the other way."

The Netherlands has begun to change its cannabis policies after decades of "looking the other way." The number of cannabis coffee shops, such as the one pictured above, has been declining in recent years.

Amsterdam is considering reclassifying marijuana or marijuana products with more than 15 percent tetrahydrocannabinol (THC) as "hard drugs." THC is a natural chemical compound found in the flowers of the marijuana plant. It produces a feeling of euphoria and a psychoactive reaction (or "high") when eaten or smoked. City officials have also asked coffee shops that were previously home to both a good Amsterdam beer and several marijuana strains to choose between selling alcohol or marijuana. Officials don't feel it's safe to mix the two, and many other countries, including the United States, feel the same. Amsterdam coffee shops are also being closed due to laws governing their closeness, or proximity, to other businesses, and no new licenses are being issued. Today, there are fewer than 200 cannabis coffee shops in the city and only about 615 nationwide. New laws passed in Amsterdam in

2011 made it illegal to grow cannabis in an indoor facility with special soil or high-grade seeds. Lawbreakers can be evicted from (forced to leave) their homes. Opponents of the new laws are concerned that enforcing the illegality of cannabis will cause the drug again to be sold in the streets, where prices may go up, and violence may occur.

China

In ancient China, cannabis was used in various ways, including to make textiles (clothing and burial shrouds), as food, as medicine, and to make paper. The earliest mention of cannabis's psychoactive effects (affecting the mind) appeared in documents found in Shanxi Province, where the Chinese character for hemp was noted, along with the differences between psychoactive cannabis and hemp. The

Medical Cannabis Research in Israel

One example of noteworthy medical cannabis research in Israel involved a 2016 study on intractable pediatric epilepsy, which affects children like Charlotte Figi (who is profiled in chapter 2). Seventy-four patients, aged one to eighteen, whose epilepsy symptoms were not improved by diet or surgery, were involved in the study. All children were treated for three to six months with high-CBD oil. Eighty-nine percent had a reduction in seizure frequency, and five reported increased seizures. With the stopping of seizures, patients were more alert, were better behaved, and experienced improvements in communication, motor skills, and the ability to sleep. The negative effects included sleepiness, tiredness, stomach pains, and irritability in the five patients who had increased seizures. Researchers in Israel are also studying cannabis as an option for people suffering from post-traumatic stress disorder and the use of cannabis to treat opioid addiction.

Emperor Shen Nung mentioned psychoactive cannabis used in a medical capacity as early as 2,000 B.C.E. Hua To, a Chinese surgeon from the second century A.D. used cannabis seeds to make an anesthetic (a substance that causes the patient to lose consciousness or feeling in an area of the body) prior to performing abdominal surgery.

Hemp has been cultivated in China for at least five thousand years. In China today, hemp is accepted, grown in large fields, and shipped to the United States, among other countries. China is one of the largest hemp growers in the world. Chinese hemp farmers want to get involved in the hemp-derived cannabidiol industry. They hope that hemp will grow in value and become a high-value cash crop. China's hemp industry is governed by the same rules as the U.S. hemp research industry and in states that allow hemp farming, meaning that industrial hemp crops must contain less than .3 percent THC. The provinces of Yunnan and Heilongjiang are major centers of hemp fiber production.

While hemp is accepted in China, marijuana, on the other hand, is not. China is strictly anti-marijuana, and many people have been arrested in the past few years for possession of cannabis. The punishments for cannabis possession in China are very strict, and often include jail time. In China, dealing drugs is punishable by execution. China's National Narcotics Control Commission reports that there were 2.5 million users of illegal drugs in China at the end of 2016, a 6.8 percent increase from 2015. China seeks to help drug addicts through traditional Chinese medicine using herbs, treatment centers, and virtual reality films which show drug users the consequences of their addictions.

Israel

Israel decriminalized the use of recreational cannabis in 2017, and it also approved the growth, manufacture, and export (sending products from one country to another) of cannabis. Cannabis research in Israel is legal and moving full steam ahead in both the government and business sectors. There are about 120 ongoing cannabis studies. They are examining the effects of cannabis on autism, epilepsy, tinnitus, psoriasis, and other medical conditions. More than five hundred companies in Israel have applied for licenses to grow, manufacture, and export cannabis products, according to Reuters.

A nurse stores medical cannabis in a nursing home in Israel.

Israel's medical cannabis program, started in 1996, is the oldest in existence. The *New York Times* reports that twenty-five thousand Israelis have medical marijuana permits for the treatment of cancer, epilepsy, and other conditions, and can obtain medicine by home delivery or through special medical cannabis dispensaries. Cannabis research is viewed as legitimately contributing to the health and well-being of Israelis. The Health Ministry's medical cannabis unit is making antibiotics from cannabis. Izun Pharmaceuticals, an Israeli drug company, has announced that it has found cannabinoid profiles that can be used to help people with Parkinson's disease and other **neurodegenerative diseases**, as well as reduce pain and increase appetite. Tikun Olam is the oldest medical cannabis clinic in Israel. It has more than nine thousand patients. The clinic's chief executive believes that the use of medical cannabis will increase dramatically due to its minor side effects and the growing acceptance of the use of cannabis in Israel and other countries. Israel has developed international partnerships with Canadian and American cannabis companies.

Beyond Israel in the Middle East

Unlike Israel, other countries in the Middle East have strict rules prohibiting the growth, possession, use, and sale of cannabis. For example, in Tunisia, anyone who is caught using or possessing cannabis receives a minimum sentence of one year in prison. Those who are caught again get up to five years. In Saudi Arabia, cannabis users can be put in jail for months or even years. Drug dealers and smugglers receive longer jail sentences, or they are executed. Cannabis is illegal in Egypt, but there is a long history of its use in Egyptian culture. Drug smugglers and dealers receive long prison sentences, and some large-scale lawbreakers are executed.

Yet, despite the strict laws in many Middle Eastern countries, cannabis is still widely used, and it is grown in many countries, including Morocco, Lebanon, and Egypt. Some countries are rethinking cannabis laws because of prison overcrowding and other factors. In Tunisia, government officials are currently debating laws that will eliminate prison terms for first- and second-time offenders caught with cannabis for personal use, and that would place more emphasis on treatment. Drug offenders (often those caught with cannabis) make up about 28 percent of the prison population in Tunisia, according to *The Economist*. The Moroccan government is considering legalizing cannabis production for medical and industrial uses.

Canada

Medical marijuana has been legal in Canada since 2001. Marijuana production is tightly controlled by the government. Patients must receive their medicine through the mail or from a courier. Dispensaries are still illegal in Canada, although many exist in major cities. They are frequently shut down by police, but continue to open or

Marchers walk in a pro-cannabis legalization parade in Canada.

reopen. Unlike in the United States, cannabis patients in Canada do not have many choices on how to consume cannabis. Edibles are illegal, as are cannabis oils and concentrates such as shatter (cannabis concentrate that looks like colored glass) and hash (a solid or resinous extract of cannabis).

The Canadian government is currently in the process of legalizing cannabis for recreational use. If the Cannabis Act is passed, recreational use of marijuana by those age eighteen or older will be allowed. Canadian residents may grow up to four plants for personal and home use, but most will be required to buy commercial cannabis from licensed cannabis cultivation companies. Growing, importing (bringing goods into one country from another), exporting (sending products from one country to another), or selling marijuana in any other instance will remain illegal. Strong laws that restrict the giving or selling of cannabis to those under the age of eighteen will also be enacted. Each Canadian province, much like U.S. states, will license and oversee the distribution and sale of cannabis, subject to federal government oversight. For example, a province may choose to increase the minimum age in its province or territory (but not lower it) or limit or expand the public places where adults can use cannabis. Under the Cannabis Act, the federal government would be required to license and regulate growing facilities. The Canadian Parliament will also have to develop breathalyzer tests for drivers and employees, and discuss international drug treaty issues that legalization may raise.

Learn more about cannabis legalization in Uruguay.

Latin America

In Latin America, Uruguay has legalized medical and recreational cannabis, and Chile and Brazil are not far behind. Uruguay was the first South American country to legalize cannabis use, cultivation, and sales in 2013. It has a history of low crime, political stability, and a higher standard of living than some Latin American countries. As of July 2017, both recreational and medical cannabis users can visit a dispensary to purchase cannabis or grow their own cannabis in their homes. The government of Uruguay is determined to prevent a cannabis tourist culture like the one that existed in Amsterdam for many years. Cannabis users must register with the government, and fingerprint scanners are used, as well as strict rules on how much cannabis can

Both recreational and medical cannabis is legal in Uruguay, a country in South America.

be bought, to prevent criminal activity and abuse. Uruguay also charges prices that are lower than those charged on the black market to encourage use of government-provided cannabis. Uruguay does not allow cannabis advertising and uses a percentage of its cannabis sales to pay for public awareness campaigns and drug addiction treatment facilities. Cannabis consumers in Uruguay, seven thousand of whom have registered with the government, can also organize **cannabis clubs** where up to forty-five people can grow ninety-nine plants for personal use. Other South American and North American countries may look to Uruguay's policies and laws to create their own in the future.

The **War on Drugs** has contributed greatly to Mexico and Latin America's increasingly tolerant view of cannabis. Residents and government officials alike hope that legalizing cannabis will reduce violent drug and cartel crime that hurts so many people in Mexico and South America. A study by Parametría in 2016 found that 29 percent of Mexicans favored cannabis legalization—an increase of 21 percent from a decade earlier. The *International Journal of Drug Policy* found that 41 percent of Mexicans want cannabis to become legal.

In 2017, Argentina and Mexico approved medical marijuana use. Chile, Panama, and Colombia have also legalized medical marijuana in an effort to provide farmers with an alternative crop and reduce drug trafficking across their nations. In much of Latin America, small amounts of cannabis have been decriminalized, reducing crime and convictions in those countries. Cannabis is still illegal in Honduras, Nicaragua, Guatemala, and Bolivia (although personal possession has been decriminalized).

United States

As of 2017, twenty-nine states and the District of Columbia permitted the use of medical cannabis. Eight states have legalized recreational cannabis for adult consumption: Alaska, California, Colorado, Maine, Massachusetts, Nevada, Oregon, and Washington. While information on cannabis sales is difficult to obtain due to federal restrictions, *Forbes* reported that North American (U.S. and Canada) marijuana sales grew 30 percent in 2016, and totaled $6.7 billion as reported by the cannabis industry research firm Arcview Market Research. The industry may earn $20.2 billion by 2021. Despite the federal government's continued uncertainty regarding marijuana legalization, states continue to legalize cannabis, with Pennsylvania, Ohio, and Arkansas recently legalizing medical cannabis. The emergence of the cannabis industry in the United States has led to strong job growth and real estate market resurgence in Colorado and other states. The U.S. cannabis industry employs 165,000 to 230,000 workers. This number could more than double in the next three to five years. Many cannabis businesses, patients, and recreational cannabis users hope that the federal government will legalize recreational and medical cannabis nationwide as Canada is preparing to do. They believe that doing so will lead to increased tax revenues for all states, more business opportunities and jobs, and medicinal access for all citizens.

A medical marijuana clinic in California. Public opinion supporting legalization of cannabis—especially for medical uses—continues to grow in the United States.

text-dependent questions

1. Which country placed hempen burial shrouds on its dead?
2. Which country was the first in the world to fully legalize recreational cannabis for production and consumption?
3. Why isn't recreational cannabis legal in every U.S. state?

research project

Choose a country and investigate its laws on cannabis, as well as its cannabis history. Compare its laws to those in the United States.

The U.S. Drug Enforcement Agency recently allowed more facilities to grow cannabis for use in medical research.

words to understand

lobbying: Seeking to influence a public official or others to change their opinion regarding a certain issue such as cannabis legalization, gun control, or environmental protection.

repeal: To get rid of a law or congressional act.

revenue: Money earned by selling products or services, or by taxing people or businesses.

tax revenue: Money earned by governments from individuals and businesses who pay taxes.

chapter 5

Changing Perceptions of Marijuana Around the World

Public opinion in America regarding the legalization of cannabis has changed in a big way since 1980. In that year, only 25 percent of Americans believed that cannabis should be legalized, according to a Gallup poll. In 2016, that percentage more than doubled—to 60 percent. This new openness to marijuana is not just happening in the United States. Fifty-one percent of Canadians surveyed by NRG Research Group in 2017 reported that they were in favor of legalization. Thirty-three percent were against legalization, and 14 percent neither favored nor were against the measure.

Sixty percent of Americans surveyed by Gallup in 2016 believed that cannabis should be legalized. They especially favored the legalization of medical cannabis.

Many European countries allow the use of medical marijuana and have decriminalized personal recreational use. In Latin America, Uruguay has legalized medical and recreational cannabis. On the other hand, countries such as Indonesia, China, Saudi Arabia, and Singapore continue to have very strong penalties (even death) for those caught using or selling marijuana.

Changing Perceptions of Marijuana in the United States

Growing support for cannabis legalization has translated into changes in marijuana laws during the last twenty years. Twenty-nine states and the District of Columbia, Puerto Rico, and Guam now permit the use of medical cannabis.

As a result of the push for marijuana legalization, the opioid crisis sweeping the United States, and a desire for healthier alternatives to pharmaceutical drugs, the medical industry in the U.S. and abroad is undergoing a major change in how it diagnoses, treats, and medicates patients. Many health care professionals and scientists support the use of medical cannabis for the treatment of pain, nausea caused by cancer and other diseases, muscle spasms caused by multiple sclerosis, poor

Recreational cannabis is legal in the American state of Massachusetts. Above, supporters of cannabis legalization attend the annual Boston Freedom Rally at Boston Common.

appetite and weight loss caused by chronic illness, seizure disorders, and Crohn's disease. Many others do not believe in the use of medical cannabis, or want further medical studies conducted before they embrace medical usage. The availability of such extensive research cannot happen in the United States until the federal government takes one of the following steps:

- Deschedules cannabis (removes it from the DEA's list of controlled substances, which are tightly regulated by the federal government because it considers them the most dangerous with a high potential for abuse and with no accepted medical use),
- Moves cannabis to a different schedule (reduces or gets rid of criminal penalties and allows health care professionals to write prescriptions for medical cannabis), or
- Allows a much larger amount of medical cannabis to be used at research facilities for medical studies.

For years, a 12-acre farm run by the National Institute on Drug Abuse (NIDA) at the University of Mississippi has been the only facility allowed by the DEA to provide cannabis for clinical research in the United States. Medical cannabis research studies have moved slowly because researchers were unable to get medical cannabis for their studies. By some estimates, applying for medical cannabis for a research study in the United States can take years.

The DEA recently announced that it would allow additional organizations to grow cannabis for research purposes. While many organizations have applied to be able to grow this cannabis, the agency says there is no set timeline to act.

Public acceptance in the U.S. regarding the use of recreational cannabis is also increasing, but not to the same degree as medical marijuana. Eight states have legalized recreational cannabis for adult use: Alaska, California, Colorado, Maine, Massachusetts, Nevada, Oregon, and Washington. Recreational marijuana legalization advocates tout the positive physical effects of the drug on users, the economic benefits (new jobs, more **tax revenue**, business growth), and the reduction of opioid abuse and overdose deaths. On the other hand, people who do not want cannabis to be legalized cite the increase in traffic accidents in states that allow recreational cannabis use, the negative effects of cannabis on youth (although recreational users must be at least twenty-one), an increase in crime and threatening of moral values, and a rise in hospitalizations and marijuana-related poisonings.

The trend continues toward more legalization—especially of medical cannabis. But it's important to keep in mind that the U.S. government's attitude toward cannabis legalization will play a major role in further legalization—or even a **repeal** of existing laws. But it will be hard to repeal existing laws because the medical and recreational cannabis industry has become a big part of the American economy. **Revenues** in the legal cannabis market were $6.6 billion in 2016, according to a report from New Frontier Data. It estimates that the legal cannabis market will create more than a quarter of a million jobs within three years. This is higher than the expected new jobs that will become available in manufacturing, utilities, or the government.

Growing Acceptance Throughout the World

Opinions about cannabis are changing in many countries as more evidence is uncovered that supports the use of cannabis as a medicine. There is also a growing trend toward the legalization, or at least decriminalization, of recreational cannabis for adults. Mexico is a good example of how opinions and laws have changed. Until 2009, the use of cannabis in all forms had been illegal. But in that year, Mexico decriminalized the possession of cannabis for those having up to five grams (0.17637 ounces) in an effort to treat possession as a public health issue rather than a criminal one. In 2015, Mexico's Supreme Court allowed an eight-year-old girl named Graciela Elizalde, who suffered from a severe form of epilepsy, to legally take a marijuana-derived oil that had drastically reduced her seizures. In 2017, Mexico legalized medical marijuana, but required that all cannabis products contain less than one percent THC—a very low percentage. THC is a natural chemical compound found in the marijuana plant that produces a feeling of euphoria and a psychoactive reaction, or "high," when eaten or smoked. Most of the Mexican people do not support the legalization of recreational cannabis. According to a 2015 poll by the Center of Social Studies and Public Opinion, 73 percent of Mexicans were against legalizing cannabis for recreational use, but 76 percent approved legalizing it for medical use. Despite the public's opposition to the legalization of recreational cannabis, recent developments show that opinions can change. President Enrique Peña Nieto, who previously opposed legalizing cannabis, said in an interview in *Cultura Colectiva,* "I'm not ruling out that in the near future marijuana will be fully legalized in Mexico. It's already occurring in other countries, particularly the United States."

Opinions about cannabis legalization continue to change throughout the world. Countries that have legalized medical cannabis in recent years include parts of the United States, Canada, Australia, Jamaica, Colombia, the Czech Republic, Spain, Portugal, Switzerland, Romania, Germany, India, Israel, Macedonia, South Africa, and Uruguay. Many more countries, including much of Latin America and Europe, have decriminalized cannabis to such an extent that law enforcement officials focus more on dangerous crimes or investigations into harder drugs such as cocaine, heroin, or methamphetamine.

But this is not the case in all countries. Laws regarding cannabis use remain restrictive in China, France, Indonesia, Nigeria, Norway, the Philippines, Japan, Malaysia, South Korea, Thailand, Poland, Saudi Arabia, Singapore, Turkey, Ukraine, the United Arab Emirates, Vietnam, and other countries.

In the coming years, the people of the world will decide for themselves whether medical cannabis can help them, or whether they choose to consume medical cannabis in their daily lives. They will also make their opinions known about the legalization of recreational cannabis. Governments will need to make big decisions regarding the legalization of both medical and recreational cannabis. Those who

Cannabis legalization supporters attend a rally in Warsaw, Poland.

Australia's Medicinal Marijuana Program

In 2016, Australia legalized medical cannabis, revising the Narcotic Drugs Act at the same time to allow cannabis to be "legally grown for medical and scientific purposes." It is also supporting and helping to fund a cannabis food program, encouraging the consumption of cannabis seeds and non-psychoactive hemp derivatives in its products. Many credit a nurse named Lucy Haslam with encouraging the government to approve the use of medical cannabis. She and her husband (a former police officer) were originally against the use of cannabis. But that changed when her son Dan was diagnosed with terminal bowel cancer. The chemotherapy treatments made him very sick, so he began using cannabis to reduce his symptoms and ease pain and nausea. His quality of life improved. Unfortunately, Dan eventually died, but Lucy and her husband began **lobbying** elected officials to legalize medical cannabis. They also launched United in Compassion, an organization that educates people about medical cannabis, as well as organized Australia's first Medicinal Cannabis Symposium. The next year, the Australian state of New South Wales (NSW) established the NSW Centre for Medicinal Cannabis Research and Innovation. Medicinal marijuana will soon be available in-country for Australian patients (the government had previously imported it on a case-by-case basis for its medical patients). While Australia works to cultivate its medical marijuana industry, it has eased laws on the import and storage of large amounts of cannabis to meet patient demand. Australia's medical cannabis prescription laws and regulations are fairly strong in an effort to keep drug abuse to a minimum. States and territories, as in Canada and the U.S., may choose the medical conditions they want to treat with cannabis. Many Australians are accepting of this more gradual approach to legalization.

support legalization hope that more countries will begin to see that the positive effects of medical cannabis outweigh the negatives. Overall, public opinion in many countries is swinging in favor of medical cannabis legalization and, to a lesser extent, recreational legalization for adults.

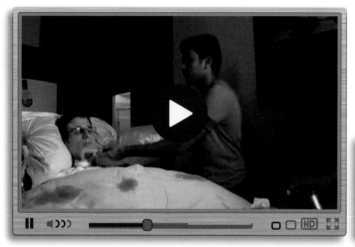

Learn about medical cannabis research in Israel and view an interview with Dr. Raphael Mechoulam, who discovered THC in cannabis and the endocannabinoid system.

Some world leaders who formerly opposed cannabis legalization are changing their opinions. For example, Mexican President Enrique Peña Nieto (right) recently said: "I'm not ruling out that in the near future marijuana will be fully legalized in Mexico."

A Closer Look at Ongoing Medical Cannabis Studies in Israel

Israel seeks to develop cannabis remedies, medications, and treatment plans to benefit patients with a variety of illnesses. In the past few years, studies have focused on cannabis-related treatments for patients with autism, pediatric epilepsy disorders, insomnia, Parkinson's disease, cancer, pain and appetite issues, and neurodegenerative illnesses. In 2015, early results from Israel's medical cannabis research study community found that cannabis can help slow cancer cell growth. Scientists at the Technion-Israel Institute of Technology in Haifa used dozens of strains (or types) of cannabis to find out how they affected the growth of hundreds of cancer cell types. This study, which might have taken years, generated results after just a few weeks: cannabis may be effective in treating brain cancers and breast cancers. The study examined whether cannabis could stop cancer cells from growing, and whether cannabis could destroy the cancer cells entirely. Scientists at Technion-Israel are partnering with Cannabics Pharmaceuticals, which makes and sells cannabis capsules that are used by cancer patients. Cannabics is a U.S.-headquartered company, but its research and development department is in Israel, where medical research into cannabis is legal. Dr. David Meiri is leading the research team on cancer and cannabis in Israel, and is also an assistant professor in biology at Technion. He recently stated that "there is a large body of scientific data which indicates that cannabinoids specifically inhibit cancer growth and promote cancer cell death." Meiri's research may someday provide effective cannabis-based treatments for those with different types of cancer around the world.

Israel is a leader in medical cannabis research. Above, medical cannabis is stored in preparation for use with nursing home patients.

text-dependent questions

1. How does the U.S. federal government feel about marijuana? If you live in a different country, how does your government feel about medical and recreational cannabis?

2. Can you name five countries that still ban the use of cannabis?

3. What are some of Dr. David Meiri's major research findings regarding cannabis and cancer?

research project

Learn more about the benefits and drawbacks of medical and recreational cannabis by visiting the websites of organizations that both support and oppose cannabis legalization.

adult-use cannabis: The recreational use of cannabis by those over the age of twenty-one.

cannabidiol (CBD): A chemical compound found in the cannabis plant that is non-psychoactive. It is known for its medical and pain relief properties.

cannabinoid: Any of various chemical compounds (such as THC) from the cannabis or marijuana plant that produces a euphoric feeling, or "high."

cannabis clubs: Marijuana growing and consumption cooperatives (a group that is owned and run by its members) that exist in countries such as Uruguay and Spain to provide cannabis users with marijuana products and a place to use those products.

cannabis strains: Varieties of cannabis plants that are developed to have different properties and potencies.

clinical trials: Experiments with unproven medications that may or may not help a patient get better.

dabbing: A somewhat controversial method of cannabis flash-vaporization. It has very strong effects on the user.

decriminalization: The legal term for getting rid of or reducing criminal charges for having or using cannabis.

delta-9-tetrahydrocannabinol (THC): A natural chemical compound found in the flowers of the marijuana plant. It produces a feeling of euphoria and a psychoactive reaction, or "high," when marijuana is eaten or smoked.

dopamine: A naturally occurring chemical in the human body that increases pleasurable feelings in the mind and body.

drug trafficking: A global illegal trade involving the growth, manufacture, distribution, and sale of substances, such as cannabis, that are subject to drug prohibition laws.

edible: A food made or infused (cooked or otherwise prepared) with cannabis extracts (portions of the plant, including seeds or flowers).

endocannabinoid system: A group of cannabinoid receptors found in the brain and central and peripheral nervous systems of mammals that help control appetite, pain, mood, and memory.

euphoria: A feeling of intense well-being and happiness.

extracts: Portions of the marijuana plant, including seeds or flowers.

hash: A solid or resinous extract of cannabis.

hemp: A cannabis plant grown for its fiber and used to make rope, textiles, paper, and other products.

ingest: To take food, drink, or another substance into the body.

lethargy: Lack of enthusiasm and energy; a common side effect of cannabis use.

Marihuana Tax Act of 1937: A marijuana taxation act that led to the prohibition of cannabis in the United States during much of the twentieth century.

marijuana: A cannabis plant that is smoked or consumed as a psychoactive (mind-altering) drug.

marijuana dispensary: A place where people can buy recreational or medical cannabis. Dispensaries are tightly controlled by the government.

marijuana oil: Liquid that is extracted from the hemp plant and placed in either capsule form or combined with foods or drinks. CBD is most commonly consumed as an oil.

medical cannabis identification card: A document issued by a state where it is legal to use medical cannabis; the card indicates that a patient may use, buy, or have medical cannabis at home, on his or her person, or both.

neuroprotectant: A substance that repairs and protects the nervous system, its cells, structure, and function.

neurotransmitter: Chemicals that communicate information in the human body.

opiates: Substances derived from the opium poppy plant such as heroin.

opium: A highly addictive narcotic drug that is created by collecting and drying the milky juice that comes from the seed pods of the poppy plant.

prohibition: The action of forbidding something, especially by law.

propaganda: False information that is created to influence people.

prosecution: The conducting of legal proceedings against someone if it is believed that they broke the law.

psychoactive drug: A drug that affects the mind.

psychosis: Detachment from reality.

receptors: Groups of specialized cells that can convert energy into electrical impulses.

repeal: To get rid of a law or congressional act.

shatter: Cannabis concentrate that looks like colored glass.

social cannabis use: The use of cannabis in social settings, whether in public or private.

tar: A toxic byproduct of cigarette or marijuana smoking.

tincture: A medicine made by dissolving a drug in alcohol, vinegar, or glycerites.

topicals: Cannabis-infused lotions, balms, and salves that relieve pain and aches at the application site on the body.

vaporizer: A device that is used to turn water or medicated liquid into a vapor for inhalation.

War on Drugs: An anti-drug campaign started in the United States in 1971 by then-president Richard Nixon. Its goal was to fight drug abuse and shipments of illegal drugs to the U.S. from Latin America, Mexico, and other places.

Index

Photo Credits

Cover: Kevin Moore | Dreamstime.com

Cover: Blvdone | Dreamstime.com

Title Page: Ints Vikmanis | Dreamstime.com

6–7: Bidouze Stéphane | Dreamstime

8–9: Leszek Wrona | Dreamstime

10: Anatoli Styf | Dreamstime.com

11: Jurgajurga | Dreamstime

13: Library of Congress

16: Peter Kim | Dreamstime

17: Randy Miramontez | Dreamstime

18: Joshua Rainey | Dreamstime

19: Ronalesa Schneider | Dreamstime.com

20: Openrangestock | Dreamstime

21: Jan Havlicek | Dreamstime

22: Spokesperson Unit of the President of Israel

29: Jaroslav Kettner | Dreamstime

30: Michael Nosek | Dreamstime

31: Roxana Gonzalez | Dreamstime

32: Jana Kleteckova | Dreamstime

34: Andreblais | Dreamstime

35: Stevanzz | Dreamstime

36: Rafael Ben Ari | Dreamstime

40: Roxana Gonzalez | Dreamstime

42: Eladora | Dreamstime

44: Jonathan Weiss | Dreamstime

47: Garudeya | Dreamstime

48: Aleksandra Lande | Dreamstime

49: Tmcfarlan | Dreamstime

51: Sbostock | Dreamstime

53: Ongap | Dreamstime.com

54: Rafael Ben Ari | Dreamstime

56: Nuvista | Dreamstime

58: Fckncg | Dreamstime

60: Zepherwind | Dreamstime

61: Teri Virbickis | Dreamstime.com

62: Mario Cupkovic | Dreamstime

63: Juan Camilo Bernal | Dreamstime

64: Ritu Jethani | Dreamstime

67: Fotokon | Dreamstime

69: U.S. Department of State

71: Rafael Ben Ari | Dreamstime

Further Reading & Internet Resources

Campos, Isaac. *Home Grown: Marijuana and the Origins of Mexico's War on Drugs*. Chapel Hill, N.C.: The University of North Carolina Press, 2014.

Hari, Johann. *Chasing the Scream: The First and Last Days of the War on Drugs*. New York: Bloomsbury USA, 2016.

Hudak, John. *Marijuana: A Short History*. Washington, D.C.: Brookings Institution Press, 2016.

Lee, Martin A. *Smoke Signals: A Social History of Marijuana: Medical, Recreational and Scientific*. New York: Scribner, 2013.

Schlosser, Eric. *Reefer Madness: Sex, Drugs, and Cheap Labor in the American Black Market*. Boston: Mariner Books, 2004.

Internet Resources

http://www.ncsl.org/research/health/state-medical-marijuana-laws.aspx: This is the official website of the National Conference for State Legislatures. It provides information on current U.S. medical cannabis laws.

https://www.drugabuse.gov/drugs-abuse/marijuana: This is the official U.S. government website for marijuana created by the National Institute on Drug Abuse (NIDA). It includes a description of marijuana and its health effects, as well as statistics and information on trends and research.

https://www.drugabuse.gov/publications/marijuana-facts-teens/want-to-know-more-some-faqs-about-marijuana: This website from the NIDA answers frequently asked questions about marijuana such: How does marijuana work? Does marijuana use lead to other drugs? What happens if you smoke marijuana? What does marijuana do to the brain?

https://www.cdc.gov/marijuana/factsheets/teens.htm: This website from the Centers for Disease Control and Prevention provides information on marijuana's effects on teens.

http://hemphistoryweek.com: Hemp History Week is an organization that is working toward hemp acceptance in the world. It is a good resource for more information about hemp farming, products, and history. It also features interviews with hemp farmers.

About the Author:

Julie Nelson is a cannabis industry consultant and freelance writer and editor, and a native Coloradan. She holds a B.A. in creative writing from the University of Colorado at Boulder, a master's in technical communication from Minnesota State University at Mankato, and is pursuing a degree in medical communication from Boston University. Julie has written and researched extensively in the areas of medical, technical, academic, and political writing. Her experience in the ever-expanding medical and recreational cannabis industry in Colorado is what drew her to this project, and the chance to spread accurate, researched, and correct information about the cannabis plant in a way that students and instructors might understand. Julie also writes short fiction, children's books, and short horror fiction, and her work has been published in numerous anthologies and online. Julie's journalism and other writing on the cannabis industry has been published in *Bust*, and online at 3C Cannabis Consulting, Mass Roots, Green Lotus Hemp, and many other websites. Julie lives in Denver, Colorado, with her family and enjoys every season to the fullest.

Video Credits

Chapter 1:

View the 1936 trailer for the marijuana propaganda film *Reefer Madness* to see how cannabis was depicted by the media and society in the 1930s.: http://x-qr.net/1H9N

This anti-drug film from the 1950s details the dangers of cannabis and heroin.: http://x-qr.net/1Dnq

Chapter 2:

Learn more about Charlotte Figi and Charlotte's Web.: http://x-qr.net/1HVX

Chapter 3:

Check out an interview with a medical cannabis farmer.: http://x-qr.net/1HqD

Chapter 4:

Learn more about cannabis legalization in Uruguay.: http://x-qr.net/1FCG

Chapter 5:

Learn about medical cannabis research in Israel and view an interview with Dr. Raphael Mechoulam, who discovered THC in cannabis and the endocannabinoid system.: http://x-qr.net/1GN0